THE LIBRARY OF
EASY PIANO
CLASSICS

THIS BOOK COPYRIGHT © 1991 BY AMSCO PUBLICATIONS
A DIVISION OF MUSIC SALES CORPORATION, NEW YORK, NY.

ALL RIGHTS RESERVED. NO PART OF THIS BOOK MAY BE
REPRODUCED IN ANY FORM OR BY ANY ELECTRONIC OR MECHANICAL MEANS
INCLUDING INFORMATION STORAGE AND RETRIEVAL SYSTEMS,
WITHOUT PERMISSION IN WRITING FROM THE PUBLISHER.

ORDER NO. AM 80151
US INTERNATIONAL STANDARD BOOK NUMBER: 0.8256.1284.5
UK INTERNATIONAL STANDARD BOOK NUMBER: 0.7119.2327.2

EXCLUSIVE DISTRIBUTORS:
MUSIC SALES CORPORATION
257 PARK AVENUE SOUTH, NEW YORK, NY 10010 USA
MUSIC SALES LIMITED
8/9 FRITH STREET, LONDON W1V 5TZ ENGLAND
MUSIC SALES PTY. LIMITED
120 ROTHSCHILD STREET, ROSEBERY, SYDNEY, NSW 2018, AUSTRALIA

PRINTED IN THE UNITED STATES OF AMERICA BY
VICKS LITHOGRAPH AND PRINTING CORPORATION

AMSCO PUBLICATIONS
NEW YORK/LONDON/SYDNEY

CONTENTS

Tango .... Albéniz 4
Deep River .... American Spiritual 7
Little David .... American Spiritual 8
Swing Low, Sweet Chariot .... American Spiritual 9
Rule, Britannia .... Arne 10
Theme *from* Solfeggietto .... C.P.E. Bach 11
Air On The G String (Suite No. 3) .... J.S. Bach 14
Arioso .... J.S. Bach 16
Sheep May Safely Graze *from* Cantata No. 208 .... J.S. Bach 18
Für Elise .... Beethoven 24
Ode To Joy *from the* Choral Symphony .... Beethoven 26
Pastoral Symphony .... Beethoven 21
Theme *from the* Fifth Symphony .... Beethoven 28
Theme *from the* Moonlight Sonata .... Beethoven 31
Theme *from the* Pathétique Sonata .... Beethoven 34
The Shepherds' Farewell *from* The Childhood of Christ ...... Berlioz 40
Themes *from* Carmen .... Bizet 42
Minuet .... Boccherini 37
Nocturne .... Borodin 48
Theme *from* Polovtsian Dances (Prince Igor) .... Borodin 45
Gaudeamus Igitur *from* Academic Festival Overture .... Brahms 56
Hungarian Dance No. 5 .... Brahms 50
Theme *from* Symphony No. 1 .... Brahms 52
Theme *from* Variations On A Theme Of Haydn (St. Anthony Chorale) ...... Brahms 54
Prelude .... Chopin 91
Tristesse Study .... Chopin 60
Trumpet Voluntary .... Clarke 57
The Cuckoo .... Daquin 65
Clair De Lune .... Debussy 68
Golliwog's Cake Walk *from* The Children's Corner .... Debussy 62
Waltz *from* Coppélia .... Delibes 70
Themes *from* La Calinda (Koanga) .... Delius 72
Tom Bowling .... Dibdin 75
Humoreske .... Dvořák 76
Theme *from* New World Symphony .... Dvořák 78
Chanson De Matin .... Elgar 81
Land Of Hope And Glory (Pomp And Circumstance) .... Elgar 84
Nimrod *from the* "Enigma" Variations .... Elgar 86
Theme *from* Pomp And Circumstance March No. 4 .... Elgar 90
Theme *from the* Cello Concerto .... Elgar 92
Dixie Land .... Emmett 89
Drink To Me Only With Thine Eyes .... English Air 94
Country Gardens .... English Air 96
Greensleeves .... English Air 95
The British Grenadiers .... English Air 98
Pavane .... Fauré 99
Berceuse .... Fauré 102
Pie Jesu *from the* Requiem .... Fauré 104
Sicilienne .... Fauré 106
Tambourin .... Gossec 108
Ave Maria .... Gounod 115
Morning *from* Peer Gynt Suite .... Grieg 110
Bourrée and Air *from* Water Music .... Handel 112
The Harmonious Blacksmith .... Handel 118
Hornpipe *from* Water Music .... Handel 120
Largo *from* Xerxes .... Handel 125
Sarabande *from* Suite XI .... Handel 122
See, The Conquering Hero Comes *from* Judas Maccabaeus .... Handel 128
Where'er You Walk .... Handel 131
Zadok The Priest .... Handel 134
I Vow To Thee, My Country (Jupiter *from* The Planets) .... Holst 138
Evening Prayer *from* Hänsel And Gretel .... Humperdinck 140
Procession Of The Sardar *from* Caucasian Sketches .... Ippolitov-Ivanov 142

Cockles And Mussels	Irish Air	137
Londonderry Air	Irish Air	144
The Minstrel Boy	Irish Air	145
Liebestraum No. 3 (Nocturne)	Liszt	146
To A Wild Rose *from* Woodland Sketches	MacDowell	149
Theme from Death In Venice (Symphony No. 5)	Mahler	152
Méditation *from* Thaïs	Massenet	154
O, For The Wings Of A Dove	Mendelssohn	156
On Wings Of Song	Mendelssohn	158
Wedding March *from* A Midsummer's Night's Dream	Mendelssohn	161
A Musical Joke	Mozart	164
Alleluia (Exultate, Jubilate)	Mozart	166
Theme from Elvira Madigan (Piano Concerto No. 21)	Mozart	170
Theme *from* Sonata In C	Mozart	173
Theme *from* Symphony No. 40	Mozart	176
Theme *from the* Clarinet Concerto	Mozart	180
Themes *from* Eine Kleine Nachtmusik (Serenade In G Major)	Mozart	181
Promenade *from* Pictures At An Exhibition	Mussorgsky	184
Barcarolle *from* Tales Of Hoffman	Offenbach	186
Can-Can *from* Orpheus In The Underworld	Offenbach	188
Canon	Pachelbel	194
Jerusalem	Parry	198
Dance Of The Hours *from* La Gioconda	Ponchielli	191
O, My Beloved Father *from* Gianni Schicchi	Puccini	200
Themes *from* The Barber Of Seville	Rossini	202
Theme *from* William Tell	Rossini	206
Melody In F	Rubinstein	209
The Elephant *from* The Carnival of the Animals	Saint-Saëns	212
The Swan *from* The Carnival Of The Animals	Saint-Saëns	214
Gymnopédie No. 1	Satie	217
Ave Maria	Schubert	219
Marche Militaire	Schubert	222
Entr'acte and Ballet Music *from* Rosamunde	Schubert	225
Serenade	Schubert	228
Theme *from the* Octet	Schubert	231
Theme *from the* Unfinished Symphony	Schubert	232
Two Songs: Rose Among The Heather *and* To Music	Schubert	234
Auld Lang Syne	Scottish Air	236
The Bluebells Of Scotland	Scottish Air	237
Charlie Is My Darling	Scottish Air	238
The Skye Boat Song	Scottish Air	239
Theme *from* Vltava (Má Vlast)	Smetana	243
The Liberty Bell	Sousa	240
Radetzky March	Strauss Sr.	246
The Blue Danube	Strauss Jr.	255
Tales From The Vienna Woods	Strauss Jr.	248
For He Is An Englishman *from* H.M.S. Pinafore	Sullivan	258
Two Tunes *from* The Mikado	Sullivan	252
Two Tunes *from* The Pirates Of Penzance	Sullivan	260
Danse Des Mirlitons *from* The Nutcracker	Tchaikovsky	263
Theme *from* Romeo And Juliet	Tchaikovsky	264
Theme *from* Piano Concerto No. 1	Tchaikovsky	266
Theme *from* Swan Lake	Tchaikovsky	269
Waltz *from* Swan Lake	Tchaikovsky	272
Chorus Of The Hebrew Slaves *from* Nabucco	Verdi	274
Grand March *from* Aida	Verdi	277
La Donna É Mobile *from* Rigoletto	Verdi	280
Themes *from* The Four Seasons	Vivaldi	282
Bridal March *from* Lohengrin	Wagner	284
Pilgrims' Chorus *from* Tannhäuser	Wagner	290
Sailors' Chorus *from* The Flying Dutchman	Wagner	287
Pavane *from* Capriol Suite	Warlock	292
All Through The Night	Welsh Air	296

Tango

Isaac Albéniz
(1860–1909)

Deep River

American Spiritual

Little David

American Spiritual

Swing Low, Sweet Chariot

American Spiritual

Rule, Britannia

Thomas Arne
(1710–1778)

Theme
from Solfeggietto

Carl Phillip Emmanuel Bach
(1714–1788)

Air On The G String
(Suite No. 3)

Johann Sebastian Bach
(1685–1750)

Andante espressivo

Arioso

Johann Sebastian Bach
(1685–1750)

Adagio cantabile

Sheep May Safely Graze

from **Cantata No. 208**

Johann Sebastian Bach
(1685–1750)

2nd time, rit. _ _ _ _Fine

Pastoral Symphony
Theme from the Third Movement

Ludwig van Beethoven
(1770–1817)

Für Elise

Ludwig van Beethoven
(1770–1817)

Andante con moto

Ode To Joy
from the Choral Symphony

Ludwig van Beethoven
(1770–1817)

Allegro

Theme
from the Fifth Symphony, second movement

Ludwig van Beethoven
(1770–1817)

Andante con moto

Theme
from the Moonlight Sonata, first movement

Ludwig van Beethoven
(1770–1817)

Adagio sostenuto

Theme

from the **Pathétique Sonata, Op. 13, second movement**

Ludwig van Beethoven
(1770–1817)

Minuet

Luigi Boccherini
(1743–1806)

D.C. Minuet al Fine

The Shepherds' Farewell

from **The Childhood of Christ**

Hector Berlioz
(1803–1869)

Themes
from **Carmen**

Georges Bizet
(1838–1875)

Theme
from **Polovtsian Dances (Prince Igor)**

Alexander Borodin
(1833–1887)

Moderato con moto

Nocturne
Theme from String Quartet No. 2

Alexander Borodin
(1833–1887)

Hungarian Dance No. 5

Johannes Brahms
(1833–1897)

Theme

from **Symphony No. 1**

Finale

Johannes Brahms
(1833–1897)

Allegro non troppo

Theme

from **Variations On A Theme Of Haydn**

St. Anthony Chorale

Johannes Brahms
(1833–1897)

Gaudeamus Igitur
from The Academic Festival Overture

Johannes Brahms
(1833–1897)

Trumpet Voluntary

Jeremiah Clarke
(1673–1707)

Andante maestoso

Tristesse Study
Op. 10, No. 3

Frédéric Chopin
(1810–1849)

Golliwog's Cake Walk

from **The Children's Corner**

Claude Debussy
(1862–1918)

Allegro giusto

8va bassa. . . . .

The Cuckoo

Louis-Claude Daquin
(1694–1772)

Vivace

D.C. al
Coda

Clair De Lune

Claude Debussy
(1862–1918)

Andante très expressif

69

Waltz
from **Coppélia**

Léo Delibes
(1836–1891)

Valse moderato

Themes

from La Calinda (Koanga)

Frederick Delius
(1862–1934)

Moderato con grazia

Tom Bowling

Charles Dibdin
(1745–1814)

Humoreske

No. 7 *from* Eight Humoreskes, Op. 101

Antonín Dvořák
(1841–1904)

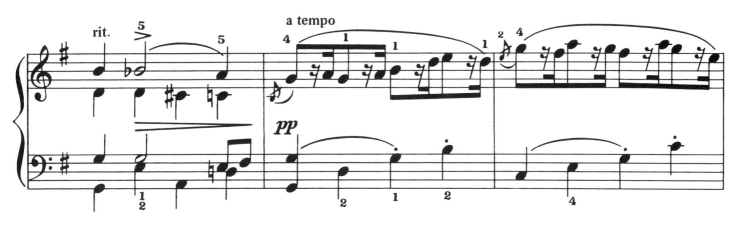

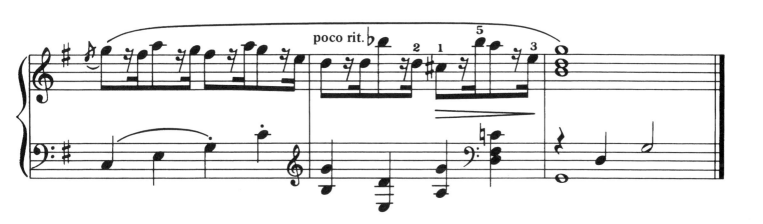

Themes
from New World Symphony

Antonin Dvořák
(1841–1904)

Allegro

Allegro risoluto

Chanson De Matin

Edward Elgar
(1857–1934)

* The original score has ornaments here.

Land Of Hope And Glory

Theme from **Pomp And Circumstance Military March No. 1**

Edward Elgar
(1857–1934)

Nimrod

from the "Enigma" Variations

Edward Elgar
(1857–1934)

Dixie Land

Daniel Decatur Emmett
(1815–1904)

Theme
from Pomp And Circumstance March No. 4

Edward Elgar
(1857–1934)

Prelude
Op. 28, No. 7

Frédéric Chopin
(1810–1849)

Theme

from the **Cello Concerto**

Edward Elgar
(1857–1934)

Drink To Me Only With Thine Eyes

English Air

Greensleeves

English Air

Country Gardens

English Air

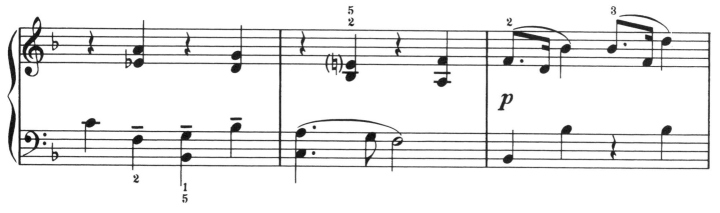

The British Grenadiers

English Air

Pavane

Gabriel Fauré
(1845–1924)

Berceuse
from **The Dolly Suite**

Gabriel Fauré
(1845–1924)

Andantino moderato

Pie Jesu
from the Requiem

Gabriel Fauré
(1845–1924)

Sicilienne

Gabriel Fauré
(1845–1924)

Tambourin

François Joseph Gossec
(1734–1829)

Morning
from Peer Gynt Suite

Edvard Grieg
(1843–1907)

111

Bourrée and Air

from **Water Music**

George Frederick Handel
(1685–1759)

Bourrée

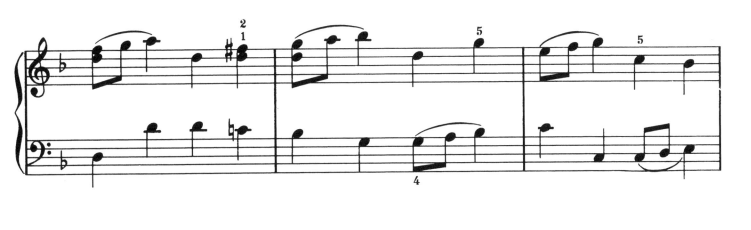

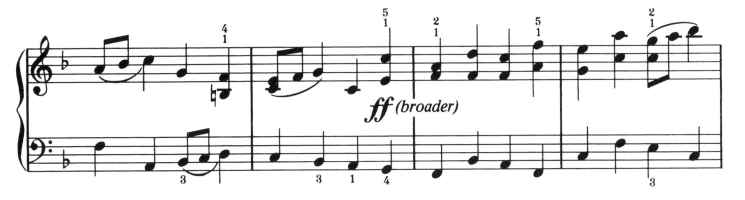

Air

114

Ave Maria
based on the First Prelude by J.S. Bach

Charles Gounod
(1818–1893)

The Harmonious Blacksmith

from Suite No. 5

George Frederick Handel
(1685–1759)

Andante cantabile

119

Hornpipe
from Water Music

George Frederick Handel
(1685–1759)

Alla Hornpipe

Sarabande

from Suite XI

George Frederick Handel
(1685–1759)

Andante con moto

Var. 1

Var. 2

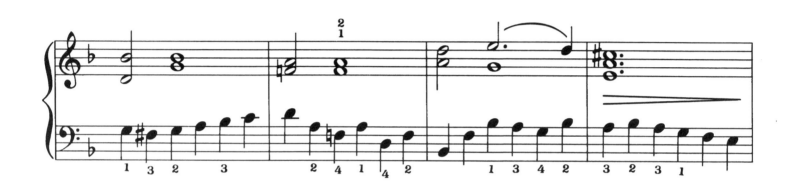

Largo
from **Xerxes**

George Frederick Handel
(1685–1759)

See, The Conquering Hero Comes

from Judas Maccabaeus

George Frederick Handel
(1685–1759)

Allegro moderato

Where'er You Walk

George Frederick Handel
(1685–1759)

cresc.

rit.

D.C.
al Fine

Zadok The Priest

George Frederick Handel
(1685–1759)

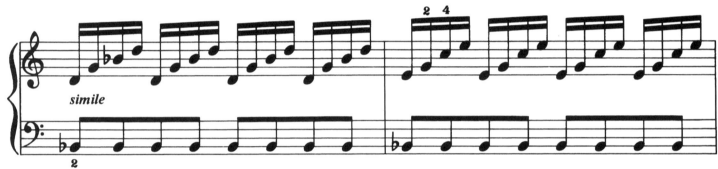

Cockles And Mussels

Irish Air

I Vow To Thee, My Country

(Jupiter *from* The Planets)

Gustav Holst
(1874–1934)

Evening Prayer
from Hänsel And Gretel

Engelbert Humperdinck
(1854–1921)

Procession Of The Sardar

from **Caucasian Sketches, Op. 10**

Mikhail Ippolitov-Ivanov
(1859–1935)

Allegro moderato, tempo marziale

Londonderry Air

Irish Air

The Minstrel Boy

Irish Air

Liebestraum No. 3
(Nocturne)

Franz Liszt
(1811–1886)

poco cresc. e agitato

8va

To A Wild Rose

from **Woodland Sketches**

Edward MacDowell
(1861–1908)

Theme from Death In Venice
(Symphony No. 5, third movement)

Gustav Mahler
(1860–1911)

Méditation
from **Thaïs**

Jules Massenet
(1842–1912)

O, For The Wings Of A Dove

from **Hear My Prayer**

Felix Mendelssohn
(1809–1847)

On Wings Of Song

Felix Mendelssohn
(1809–1847)

* *If desired, the original L.H. figuration may be used:* etc.

Wedding March
from A Midsummer's Night's Dream

Felix Mendelssohn
(1809–1847)

A Musical Joke
K. 522, fourth movement

Wolfgang Amadeus Mozart
(1756–1791)

Alleluia

from the motet **Exultate, Jubilate (K. 165)**

Wolfgang Amadeus Mozart
(1756–1791)

Allegro non troppo

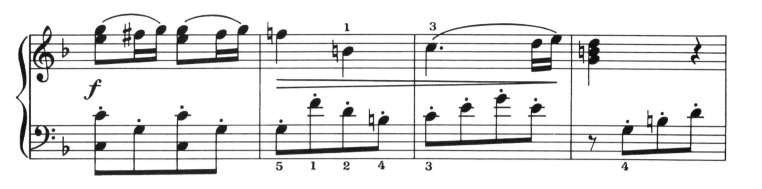

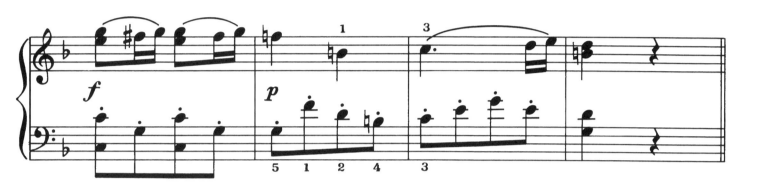

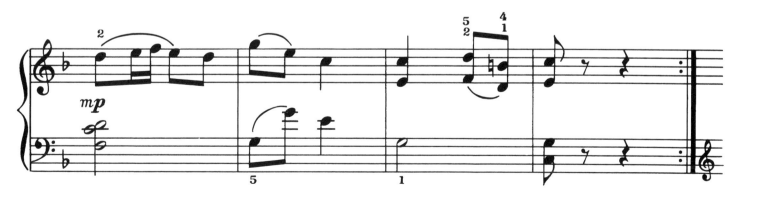

168

Theme from Elvira Madigan
(Piano Concerto No. 21, K. 467, second movement)

Wolfgang Amadeus Mozart
(1756–1791)

D.C. al Coda

Coda

Theme

from Sonata In C (K. 545, first movement)

Wolfgang Amadeus Mozart
(1756–1791)

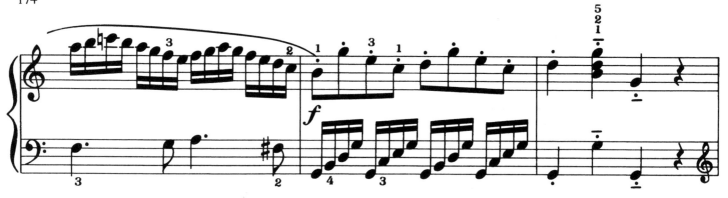

Theme

from **Symphony No. 40, first movement**

Wolfgang Amadeus Mozart
(1756–1791)

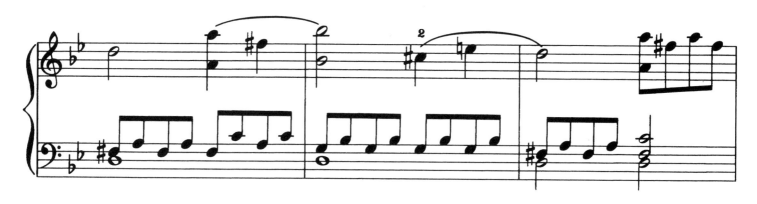

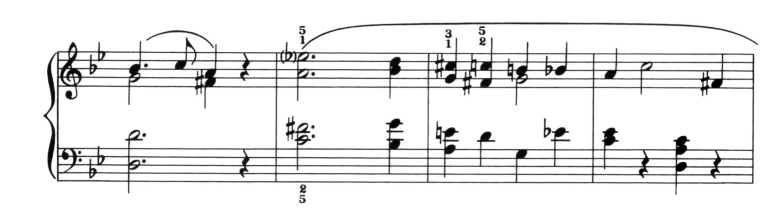

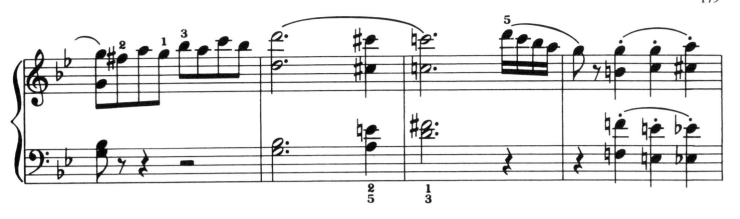

Theme
from the Clarinet Concerto

Wolfgang Amadeus Mozart
(1756–1791)

Themes

from **Eine Kleine Nachtmusik**

(Serenade In G Major (K. 525), first movement)

Wolfgang Amadeus Mozart
(1756–1791)

Promenade
from Pictures At An Exhibition

Modeste Mussorgsky
(1839–1881)

Barcarolle

from Tales Of Hoffman

Jacques Offenbach
(1819–1880)

D.S. al Fine

Can-Can

from Orpheus In The Underworld

Jacques Offenbach
(1819–1880)

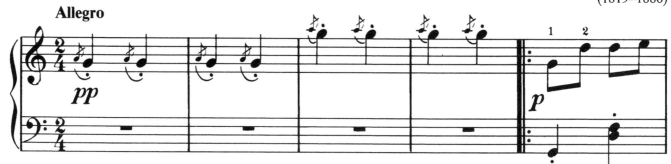

Dance Of The Hours

from **La Gioconda**

Amilcare Ponchielli
(1834–1886)

DANCE OF THE HOURS OF DAY

ENTRANCE OF THE HOURS OF NIGHT
Moderato

p espressivo

DANCE OF ALL THE HOURS
Con molto brio

Canon

Johann Pachelbel
(1653–1706)

Con 8va ad lib. . . . .

Jerusalem

Charles Parry
(1848–1918)

O, My Beloved Father

from **Gianni Schicchi**

Giacomo Puccini
(1858–1924)

Themes
from The Barber Of Seville

Gioacchino Rossini
(1792–1868)

Theme

from **William Tell**

Gioacchino Rossini
(1792–1868)

Melody In F
Op. 3, No. 1

Anton Rubinstein
(1829–1894)

210

The Elephant

from The Carnival of the Animals

Camille Saint-Saëns
(1835–1921)

The Swan

from The Carnival Of The Animals

Camille Saint-Saëns
(1835–1921)

Gymnopédie No. 1

Erik Satie
(1866–1925)

Lent et douloureux

Ave Maria

Franz Schubert
(1797–1828)

221

Marche Militaire

Franz Schubert
(1797–1828)

Allegro vivace

Entr'acte and Ballet Music

from **Rosamunde**

Franz Schubert
(1797–1828)

I. Entr'acte

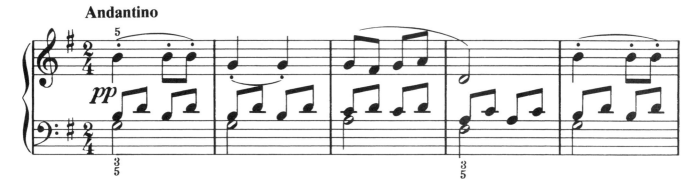

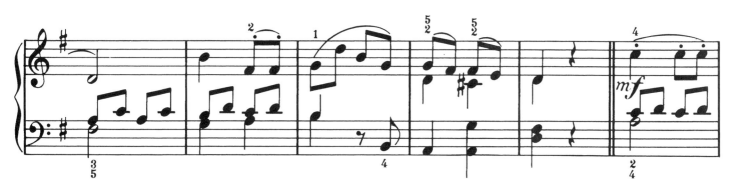

II. Ballet Music

Andantino

Fine

Serenade

Franz Schubert
(1797–1828)

Theme
from the Octet

Franz Schubert
(1797–1828)

Theme

from the Unfinished Symphony

Allegro moderato

Franz Schubert
(1797–1828)

Two Songs

Franz Schubert
(1797–1828)

I. Rose Among The Heather

II. To Music

Auld Lang Syne

Scottish Air

The Bluebells Of Scotland

Scottish Air

Moderato

Charlie Is My Darling

Scottish Air

The Skye Boat Song

Scottish Air

The Liberty Bell

John Philip Sousa
(1854–1932)

Theme

from Vltava (Má Vlast)

Bedrich Smetana
(1824–1884)

244

Radetzky March

Johann Strauss
(1804–1849)

Fine

cresc.

D.S. 𝄋 *al Fine*

Tales From The Vienna Woods

Johann Strauss
(1825–1899)

Two Tunes

from **The Mikado**

I. The Flowers That Bloom In The Spring

Arthur Sullivan
(1842–1900)

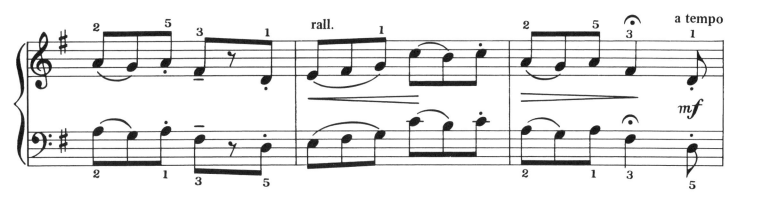

(Ped. _ _ _ _ _ _ _ ⌐)

II. Willow, Tit-Willow

Andante espressivo

(Ped. . . . .)

The Blue Danube

Johann Strauss
(1825–1899)

For He Is An Englishman

from H.M.S. Pinafore

Arthur Sullivan
(1842–1900)

Moderato

Two Tunes

from **The Pirates Of Penzance**

Arthur Sullivan
(1842–1900)

I. Poor Wand'ring One

II. The Policeman's Song

Danse Des Mirlitons

from **The Nutcracker**

Peter I. Tchaikovsky
(1840–1893)

Theme
from Romeo And Juliet

Peter I. Tchaikovsky
(1840–1893)

Theme
from Piano Concerto No. 1, first movement

Andante non troppo e molto maestoso

Peter I. Tchaikovsky
(1840–1893)

Theme
from Swan Lake

Peter I. Tchaikovsky
(1840–1893)

Waltz

from Swan Lake

Peter I. Tchaikovsky
(1840–1893)

Tempo di valse

Chorus Of The Hebrew Slaves
from **Nabucco**

Giuseppe Verdi
(1813–1901)

276

Grand March

from Aida

Giuseppe Verdi
(1813–1901)

La Donna É Mobile

from **Rigoletto**

Giuseppe Verdi
(1813–1901)

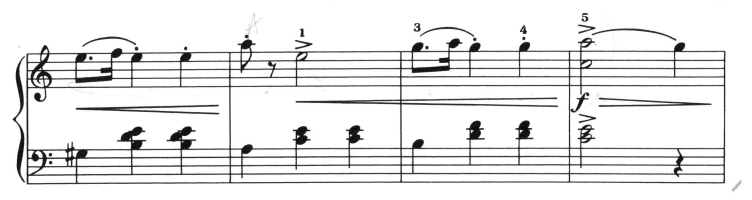

Themes

from The Four Seasons

I. Spring

Antonio Vivaldi
(1685–1741)

II. Autumn

Bridal March

from **Lohengrin**

Richard Wagner
(1813–1883)

Moderato con moto

286

Sailors' Chorus

from **The Flying Dutchman**

Richard Wagner
(1813–1883)

Pilgrims' Chorus
from Tannhäuser

Richard Wagner
(1813–1883)

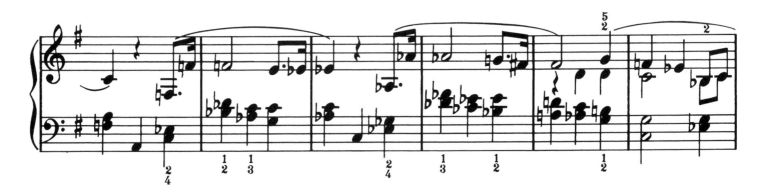

Pavane
from Capriol Suite

Peter Warlock
(1894–1930)

All Through The Night

Welsh Air

Moderato

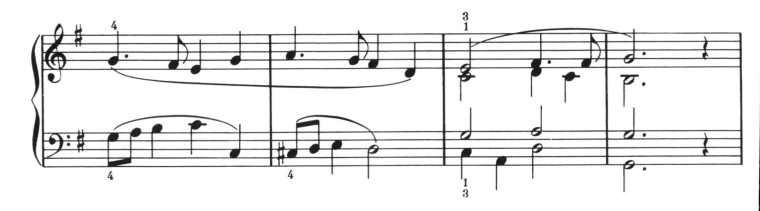

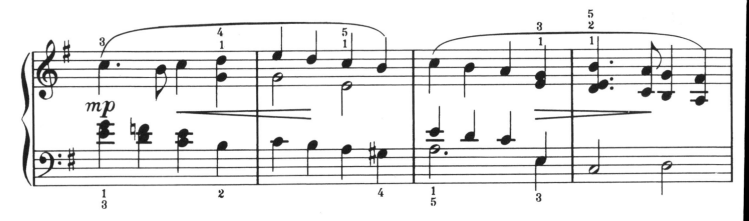